Bluing

poems by

C.W. Buckley

Finishing Line Press
Georgetown, Kentucky

Bluing

Copyright © 2018 by Christopher W. Buckley
ISBN 978-1-63534-655-8 First Edition
All rights reserved under International and Pan-American Copyright Conventions. No part of this book may be reproduced in any manner whatsoever without written permission from the publisher, except in the case of brief quotations embodied in critical articles and reviews.

ACKNOWLEDGMENTS

It Comes Back, Just as It Was first appeared in *Rock & Sling | a journal of witness*, Volume 12, Issue 2, 2018

The Garden at Sunset first appeared in *Tiferet: A Journal of Spiritual Literature*, Spring/Summer 2018

The Older Woman first appeared in *Bay Area Poets Coalition Anthology 23*, April 2002

Sea Cliff Scaled first appeared in the *Lummox Journa*l, ALL POETRY issue, April 2002

Publisher: Leah Maines
Editor: Christen Kincaid
Cover Art: C.W. Buckley
Author Photo: Tara Gimmer
Cover Design: Elizabeth Maines McCleavy

Printed in the USA on acid-free paper.
Order online: www.finishinglinepress.com
       also available on amazon.com

      Author inquiries and mail orders:
           Finishing Line Press
            P. O. Box 1626
      Georgetown, Kentucky 40324
              U. S. A.

Table of Contents

The World to Come 1

Crosswalk Ethics 3

Sea Cliff Scaled 4

The Physics of Sitting Alone 5

As Far as the East Is from the West 6

Jeremiad 7

Selective Advantage 8

The Older Woman 9

The Integrity of Ice 10

Winter Train, Looking Back 11

Like Trees Walking 12

Buyer's Remorse 13

Dining Out 15

It Comes Back, Just as It Was 16

Tuyshtak 18

A Walk in the Rain 19

Flicker 21

Cafe Campagne 23

The Garden at Sunset 24

Edward Weston 25

For
Rosie, Nicholas, and Marcus
for giving me my voice

With thanks to
Easy Speak Seattle
for giving me your ears

THE WORLD TO COME

The world is getting smaller
At least the one that matters
Most

The one I remember
The one that seemed so big
When I was
Not
And now seems only
Strange

Pictures of Janis Joplin
Before I was
Born
And she was
Gone
Recall the loud and shaggy world
Dying in my infancy
Living
Only in photographs and memory

How new, how free
She must have felt
Did they know then what they had already given
Away?
There are many words for losing it all
Freedom was never one of them

The word they were looking for is
Time
It's on my side
For now
And when the world is small enough
It will be
On its own

It's not the things we lose, you see
But the fragments of the familiar
That remain
Unused and perplexing
To all save those who remember

Like Mrs. Stewart's Bluing
Which my great-grandmother used without a second thought
Doing laundry, to trick the eye into seeing
White
Still there, yet
Unknown to all, except for restoring
Faded jeans

Looking around, I wonder
What obvious thing will be an artifact
Next?
A light bulb? A radio?
A song?
A child?

I will be their ambassador to the world
To come
Ask
And I will tell you
What they are for

CROSSWALK ETHICS

This fiction we share
Is the thing that keeps us alive
The pretense that two white stripes
Painted parallel indeed
Comprise a bridge to safety
Alongside threatening traffic

Should you walk the line
Or I straddle its twin
At what point does our contract collapse?
Does it really require tragic collision
And burning sirens to call to mind one basic fact?
That staying inside the lines
Is not nearly so vital a skill
As discerning when to step between them

SEA CLIFF SCALED

Stone-faced seals
On a sidewalk portal
Protect your homes
With condescending quiet.
All I have to bar my door
At the other end of the street
Is a squeaky iron gate.

Which do you suppose works better?

All your money
Could not get you past the bars
Into my rented room
But every week
The unbroken pavement
We share
Carries me through your mortgaged border
Onto the beach
Where even the mongrel pigeons
Glow tangerine at dusk.

THE PHYSICS OF SITTING ALONE

Suddenly, a seat is free
The man who survived
A deadly choice of two strangers
Stakes his claim
Across the bus

The balance restored
All sit unpaired and whole

What weak force or strange attractor
Must act in unseen, quantum ways to
Reverse the poles?

On that day when
Strangers on an empty bus,
Abhorring the vacuum of the vacant seat,
Deny the insult of solitude
Galaxies will collide and strip themselves
Arm from spiraling arm
Into new and brilliant complexities

Smaller than before
But all the more
Brilliant in the dark

AS FAR AS THE EAST IS FROM THE WEST

Francis the poor converted a wolf
the hunter redeemed, a village fed
Now the man hears our sapient prayer
and a lupine skull lies grinning in state
Both courting wisdom, dancing above us

Heavy cries for peace fall down cemetery walls
Haunting mission daylight, vertigo phantoms
Prophesy tomorrow's bombing and the dead
to the whitewashed silence of mestizo tombs
All denouncing folly, gnawing at our bones

A march turns parade outside in the park
the rally a carnival, causes unknown
Ravers get down for some fun in the grass
lapping at cold green helados from jingling pushcarts
Few seeking conscience, settling for play

Grief in truth is no call to war
the one thing needful, mourning becomes us
Yet the sense of the wolf calls out to the stars
There is no peace not purchased from death
Left and right echoing, burying worn paths

A barbarian saint now howls in the east
by faith converted, conscripted by force
The dog-head soldier submitted to Rome
but snarled at its gods with faces like men
So dying a martyr, uniting all flesh

JEREMIAD

Khaki in San Francisco, then jeans
All Seattle's flannel, now high-tech fleece
Unto both angels I do cry
Wool!
Warmth!
Caps for all
And all that covers
Our mutual cool

SELECTIVE ADVANTAGE

The robin's breast, once flushed
Now wraps vitality in the rustic brown
That coats the edge of autumn

From mulberry's falling applause
To the new restraint of the unemployed
All things discover safety in the somber
And question at last the violence of spring's memory

Not brilliant at all
The hues that once proclaimed their mating worth
Lure nothing but extinction now
Skulking in its rumored bonestrewn cave

It is those most fit to scarcity
Can thrive in this dull climate
The drab and out-of-season born
Take color for a gift
And give it back, enriched

There, beneath Macy's first Christmas glow
Comes a stranger, recognized in a crowd:
The old gray postman with the drooping eye
And together with festive neon and the rain
He conjures warm thoughts of marked parcels and twine

And then is gone, unsmiling
Still, his presence here before Thanksgiving
Would signal that even he must make an early start
To find the one true gift
Worthy of some special other who, blushing
Meets his gaze

THE OLDER WOMAN

She scans her pages
Windblown and fading
With a raptor's proud survey
And like the bird, blinks once
Sensing she is watched
And probing why

Her sharp features turn
Into the current of my gaze
Then sternly to the hunt return
Despite my smile
Assured, not unkind

There is no shared resource
In the nature of hawks
No common rest
Save in the détente
Of knowing the other
Will pass yours by

In the wild nothing that survives
Is curious like a man
Observing a bird of prey
No taking in of plumage
And other signs of years
To wonder how and where they were spent
And with whom

Only the call of the very young
And the sight of a brightly colored coat
Can provoke a guardian smile
Like the one that escapes
When a little girl flies by

THE INTEGRITY OF ICE

Cold enough to maintain
    Though not congeal afresh
Ice concedes a smoky sigh
    With the morning guard
        Puffing his cigarette where no one can see

Soon tourists and lovers will come out to play
    Gliding over sublimating pleasure
That mimics the risk of a breakthrough pond
    Yet with no more depth
    Than the wireless logo inches below

Depth was overrated anyway
    Security much preferred
Or so I thought
    When I first turned to ice
    For comfort

But a California freeze is forced
    Even in December
I just felt the condenser fail from the strain
    And with unbidden flush of love's recall
    Realize now the catastrophic thaw must come

WINTER TRAIN, LOOKING BACK

Did you know then
That night of a thousand Santas
When all the town turned out
In red
And I
Warm with chocolate
Waited near the station?

Could you hear my prayer
Hidden in the way the children
Surged around us, or perhaps
In my laugh
Once the clerk mistook your niece's gift for
One of our own?

How I hoped then
It was the same
You whispered, settling
Later into the chapel's dark
Together with me
And the music, after dinner
Once I'd left the longing tracks
Empty behind me

LIKE TREES WALKING
After Mark 8:24

Like trees
Like trees walking
Nothing can ever just be
What it is

Not yet a man, I see
In stages only what I am shown

Once downed and drowning
I will rise, embraced—or so they say
My life vest cushion until that hour
Merely a pain in my ass

Spit in my face, then, if that's what it takes
Only let me see the end
The where and the why
Full-grown

I struggle against the what
Every action, the trial
Every word, the last
Every one, the adversary

Never the who you conceive
Growing, perhaps, only unearthed
Like trees
Like trees walking

BUYER'S REMORSE

Even as I set the trap
I hope that third mouse will be
The last
With the rains to come
It isn't right their blood should spot
The floor of our garage
But necessary
If they are not to establish
Their winter nest

Needful, even
To offer up my regret
My thanks
For their relinquishing
What I take now for my family:
A life together in this place
This high place,
Valley-borne
Their small participation in it
Cut short for ours

Much like
The rabbits strewn cold
Before Dougherty Station
In the morning traffic
Passing
Pushed from one field to the next
By yellow steel
Once the ranchers sold

There is no crime to this regret
As I place the sprung trap
In its grocery plastic shroud
No affront to the mortgaged
In my offering account
Wheeling my bin
To the moist and newly poured curb
Merely a recognition
Of the transhuman here

An honoring of the truth
That what once was, gave way
For me, for mine
As will we all, to what is
Next to come

DINING OUT

Separate with empty places set
She with white hair permed perfect
And he for the most part unremarkable
Together conjure sounds of Artie Shaw
The smell of cigarettes when smoke was classy
And an ache in my own chest
Broken between the two

IT COMES BACK, JUST AS IT WAS

Suddenly it leapt, vaulting
over my head from the place
where it slept on my back

Only then did I notice
the fury, the fatigue I had carried
as it scampered into the brush

My spoiled pack came undone
and every ration tin I hurled
at its head missed completely

So I fled the forest
terrified, rather than face its shaggy
band of brothers slinking around behind me

Surely this time I had driven it off
once and for all, or so it seemed
when safe at home I made my coffee

A few sips only, piping hot
and there it was, sniffling
beside my open door

Asking me, pleading really
"Have you—did anybody—
has nothing been heard—about me?"

How it shocked me, gently sobbing
with hand upraised, like a boy
hit much too often

"I am used to it," a stammer
before a flood of tears, "Tell me, is all the world
as cold and dismal a place as this?"

And moved with pity
for once, not anger
I hoisted him, sighing, high upon my shoulders

TUYSHTAK

Diablo, Mount—mountain 3849 feet (1173 meters) high at the northern end of the Diablo Range of central California (Merriam-Webster)

The day I first saw you
Snow had fallen on Tuyshtak
Its mysterious dark edged fresh with bright winter
Like you, my son
And the heartbeat that sounds from your mother's womb

That was something I had never seen
This mountain called Diablo
Did once burn, ringed in orange summer
Grass fires
A corona flickering against the stars

I promise you now that here
Nothing of the Devil belongs
On these sloped shoulders rests a name, beyond seasons
Almost forgotten
In this Fallen world

Come safely to us, my little one
Come down where it is warm
Let us tell you your secret name
And you
Spring forth into the center of our world

A WALK IN THE RAIN

Most people do not know
There is only one way to walk in the rain
You're probably doing it wrong yourself
So pay attention

First, take off your coat
A wool sweater
Collarless will suffice
The cold pooling between your shoulders
Is thrilling
But wet feet are miserable
So wear good shoes

Be sure to forget your umbrella
And stand beneath an awning if it is dark
For at least five minutes
Paying attention to the way water
Falling flashes mustard or mango
between the sky's indigo
and the halogen bulb above you

Breathe deeply to moisten your lungs
Let your calves get slightly damp in long pants
Now, you're ready

Walk forward, shoulders back
And keep an even stride, arms swinging
Chest out, head up
You'll know you're doing it right
When something clammy drips off your earlobe
And your hair is plastered to your skull

This is good

Notice it is true for everyone
Even the ones darting like hermit crabs
From one shelter to the next

Do not be like them

Do not hunch over pretending you are dry
Do not run
The rain is already there and besides
You will splash and remember
What I said about wet feet

Look like you know where you are going
And do not wipe your face
Remember to blink

Only once you've reached your destination
Should you run your hands back through your hair
And stamp off the excess
At the door jamb

Enjoy the warmth now
As you did the chill a moment before
Taking pleasure in having taught the others
The difference between rain and bad weather

FLICKER

It is simpler to write of God
Than of the songs his birds
Can sing

He at least is One
And they so very many

Only in these last times
Do they astound
Having sounded, nameless
All the days of my life

Moving now, late in my season
All the birds are strange
And stop me on the street
With urgent calls
I cannot afford to ignore

These are not my childhood birds
No mere blackbirds
Or dull, uncrested jays
These are someone else's ordinary
All flit and titter
Dark-breasted and many

Others, unrevealing, haunt me
From some not-too-distant eave
So I look away
And live

Falling short of Adam's charge
I have named only one
A faithful visitor, and clever

The Flicker
A woodpecker wise enough
To toil in the dust of the earth
And not the trees
Long-billed and speckled
Like soiled ermine
And totally unremarkable in its song

CAFE CAMPAGNE

I should have turned
Around the day
We met for lunch and champagne

Perspective and the Sound
Tempted with distance and
You caught me in the photographic act

A sign, a gull
Distant Olympics aligned
Seeming an eternity
But in truth collapsed
Once stolen by my lens

Nothing at all
In your steep embrace, and my world
Magnified in your light

THE GARDEN AT SUNSET

The man raised hard-packed earth in a patch around his ankles
Clearing knotted ivy-root with a dull pick-axe
That something yet unborn to him may take root and grow

An unruly hedge that rained juniper's blue-flame berries once
On the heads of his long-ago boys, he trimmed
Back that morning to three trunks, austere and slender as saplings

He worked a symmetry adhering to some unspoken rule of gardeners
When he unearthed a wonder: a sphere, curiously light,
Of stone he imagined might contain a geode

One spelunk! of his heavy tool into that tiny crystal cave
Would deliver its hues unto the sun at last
But he decided against it, fearing lumbar pain and the mess

Besides his wife expected the yard raked clean by dusk.
He tossed the orb, arcing it over gravel to lawn
Almost smelling the rising green to spread from where it came to rest

EDWARD WESTON

I do not write about the sea
Or mottled whorls of stone near sand
Neither kelp, nor cypress
Not even a dead pelican

I only write about the eternity of these things
The way illumination inspires them to film
To print, to mind
And back now into living word

A fourth generation West Coast native, C.W. Buckley lives and works in Seattle with his family, returning to put down roots in the Pacific Northwest after his great-grandfather passed through on his way to the Yukon. After graduating with a degree in Human Biology from Stanford University, Buckley earned a master's degree in Religion at the Claremont School of Theology, during which time he served two years as an interfaith chaplain at the Stanford and Lucile Packard Children's Hospitals. After a long career in corporate communications, he now works in market development for a top professional services firm.

As a reader, he resonates with the harsh echoes of the natural world and the language of faith in the writings of the West Coast "Inhumanists" of the mid-20th Century, like Robinson Jeffers and William Everson. Buckley's voice emerges from that shared landscape, but observes instead that the coastal wilds they set to verse a century ago are today's gentrifying neighborhoods and conservation projects. Corporate by day, Catholic by faith, his writing explores geek culture, conscience, faith, and fatherhood.

Reading regularly at Easy Speak Seattle in that city's northeast, his work has also appeared in *Timberline Review, Raven Chronicles Journal, Rock & Sling | a journal of witness, Tiferet: A Journal of Spiritual Literature, Lummox Journal, POESY Magazine,* and *the Bay Area Poets Coalition* anthology. You can follow him as @chris_buckley on Twitter.

www.ingramcontent.com/pod-product-compliance
Lightning Source LLC
LaVergne TN
LVHW041515070426
835507LV00012B/1586